SHARAM

EDITED BY
Shahed & Emma

TALIA

BEYOND ZEN

SHARAM

Edited by: Shahed & Emma
Paperback 1st Edition
Published in 2025 by:

Talia, Friends of Existence, Inc.
Website: www.taliafriends.org
Email: talia@taliafriends.org

Copyright © 2025 by Talia, Friends of Existence, Inc.
ISBN 978-0-9600047-6-8

All rights reserved.

No part of this book may be reproduced, stored in a retrieval system, or transmitted in any form or by any means, electronic, mechanical, photocopying, recording or otherwise, without the prior written permission of the publisher.

Many thanks to Melina H and Chris P for their invaluable help.
Cover Art & Paintings: Sharam
Page Layout & Book Design: No Mind Design

MORE BOOKS
by Sharam

order now on:
Sharam.org

Simple Is Deep

Gentleness Works

A Monk's View of Life

Clarity for Your Day

Don't Beat Yourself Up

You Are Your Happiness

The Book of Existence
Part One

Mysticism
The Psychology of Love

Happiness
The Essence of Your Being

Decoding Love
Understanding is Compassion

From Negativity to Joy

The Power of Let-Go

Happiness
The Name of Our Soul

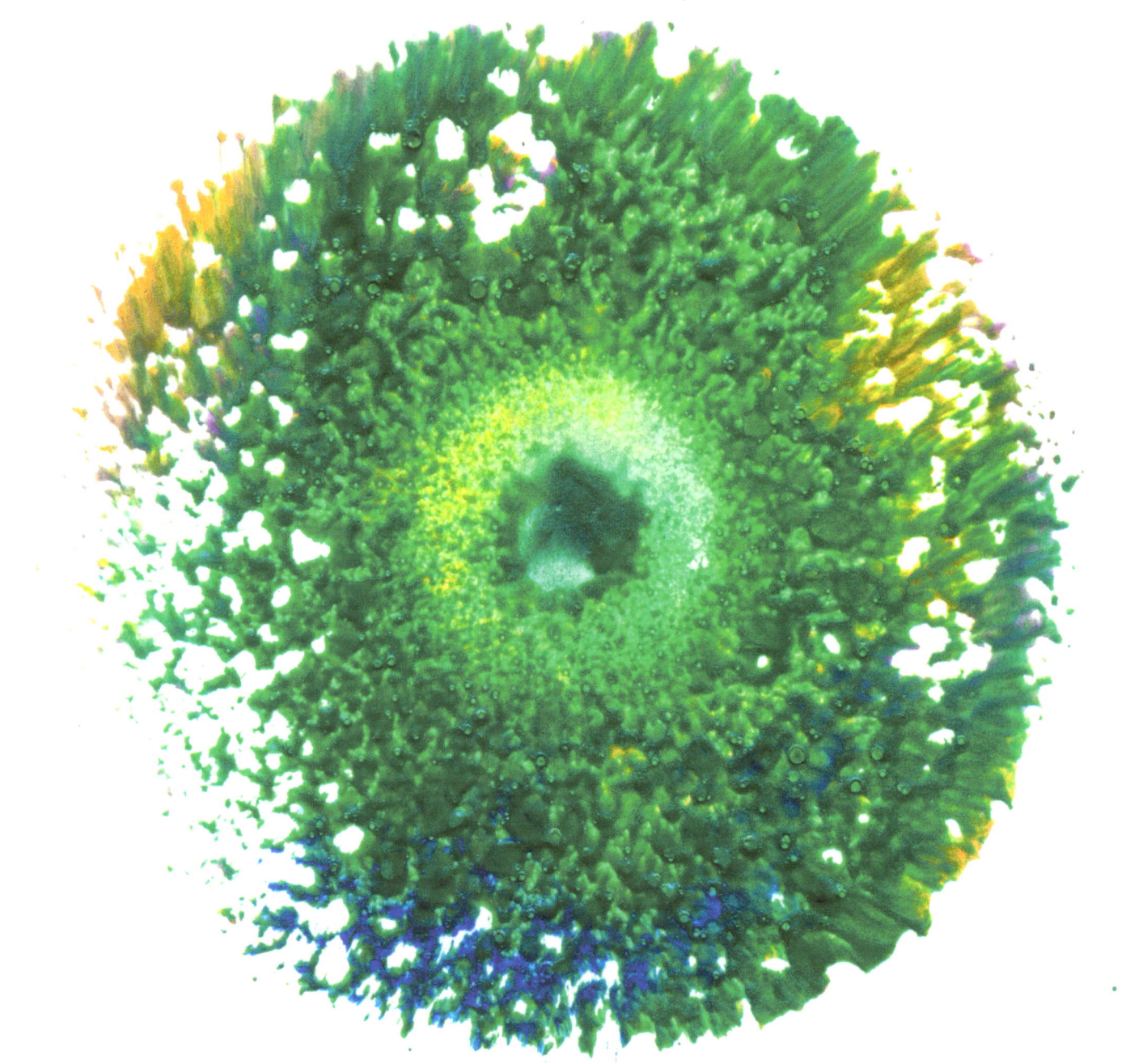

INTRODUCTION

"Whatever happens, whatever is here, is Existence. We can only understand Existence when we are not in the mind, when we are not in the past or future. Understanding Existence requires us to be here and now and whenever we are in the here and now, we laugh and feel good. We are happy."

— *Sharam*

Humans are very strong, but just as this strength can be helpful to our well-being, it can be destructive as well. For example, we suffer as a child—a parent sends us to our room for being angry or is constantly telling us in one way or another that we need to be better or different. Whatever it is, it makes us unhappy, but we get used to this suffering. We become strong in relation to this suffering, and we bear with it our whole lives. This suffering goes into our subconscious, which means we are not aware of it anymore. Maybe we feel guilty for not being better, or more successful, or have low self-esteem, but we think this is how life is supposed to be. We accept our suffering as normal.

But then we blame others for our suffering. We don't take responsibility for our actions, reactions or anything for that matter. This causes us to suffer even more because we can't change others, and if we are blaming, we are not looking at ourselves, so we stay a child. We stay immature, and when we are immature, we suffer a lot in life. If we don't blame, we become mature. We see ourselves and in doing so we become free.

All humans, in one way or another, have been mistreated as children. Then we grow up and feel the need to defend ourselves over the smallest things. But when we become defensive, we lose our ability to understand. We do not allow higher qualities to arise in us to help us understand. We immediately start fighting with the other person instead of being open to hearing their criticism, paying attention to it, and trying to understand it. We do not allow criticism to help us look at ourselves. We totally miss looking at ourselves, because we are busy defending or fighting. Basically, defending is fighting. Instead of using criticism to grow, we think of the other as rude, negative, and no good. "They are offensive, how dare they say or do this to me?"

Let's say we are in the second chakra. By cleaning our second chakra, we expand the second chakra of the universe, because the universe has seven chakras, seven levels just like us. If we grow, the universe grows with us at that level. We grow when we come to the moment. So when we come to the here and now, we expand the layer of the universe we are in.

The idea of mind over matter applies to the body deeply. Mind affects the body. The body follows the mind all the time. For example, getting sick or being happy or afraid, all come from the mind running the show. Mind is the commander. The soul is much more subtle than the mind. It runs the whole Existence. The soul is very gentle and wise and advanced. Because it is gentle, it does not interfere with the work of the mind. The mind wants to manage and control not only the body, but everything. Unfortunately, when the mind takes over, people fight. All the wars in the world have happened because the mind has taken over. In understanding, we use the mind as a servant to the soul. That is why understanding is so high. Understanding always gives us the feeling of joy and freedom.

The mind only deals with a very limited planet called Earth. But through the spark plugs of the soul, we connect to the whole universe, which is just extreme fun. It makes us so excited. Excitement is condensed energy of fun exploding. It is better than any other kind of explosion.

When a question is very strong, it comes from the fifth chakra. Questions that are a dime a dozen come from the mind.

The mind is there to help us grow. It does so by going to extremes. By going to extremes, it creates many negative situations. It creates positive situations also, but in general the mind focuses on the negative. To grow we need to go deeper than the mind, because the mind only creates problems. Unfortunately, today most people are driven by their minds. We live in a society that puts its value on the mind. We are not exposed to the incredible value of our soul and how to access it. With the mind, problems only get resolved on a very superficial level, so they will likely pop up again soon. They might have a slightly different shape or color, but the problem will be the same. With deeper understanding, we access the soul, where problems truly get resolved.

When our full focus is on the mind, it takes over and we are no longer subtle enough to be in touch with our soul. Our mind contains only what we have learned. It is not original and has nothing to do with the real us. Compassion comes from the soul and without the soul, the mind becomes very cruel. The soul is generous because it is compassionate. The mind is only fair. It has no generosity. A very condensed mind has a lot of negativity, and too much negativity turns into cruelty.

 Mind is a mechanism to defend the self, and defending the self leads to fighting because we close ourselves, which creates separation. When people separate, they don't feel safe. They have a lot of fear, which creates a lot of negativity, which turns into cruelty. When you work on yourself, the mind becomes less intense because working on the self means focusing on compassion and love. You may still get upset with others, but your upset will be mild. It won't turn to hate or wanting revenge. The mind feels more relaxed and with this relaxation, your higher self will begin to be in charge. Understanding the self connects us to our real self. So the more we understand ourselves, the more we are in touch with our soul. Another way to get in touch with the soul is to meditate. Meditation helps relax the mind, but understanding can be faster.

Mind has two parts, male and female, and they are both unstable alone. All female emotions, like being upset, come from the second chakra, and all male emotions, like hostility and aggression, come from the third chakra. So anything negative that comes from the mind comes from the lower chakras and is therefore low quality. It is only when the male and female energy join and become one that we come from a higher quality energy.

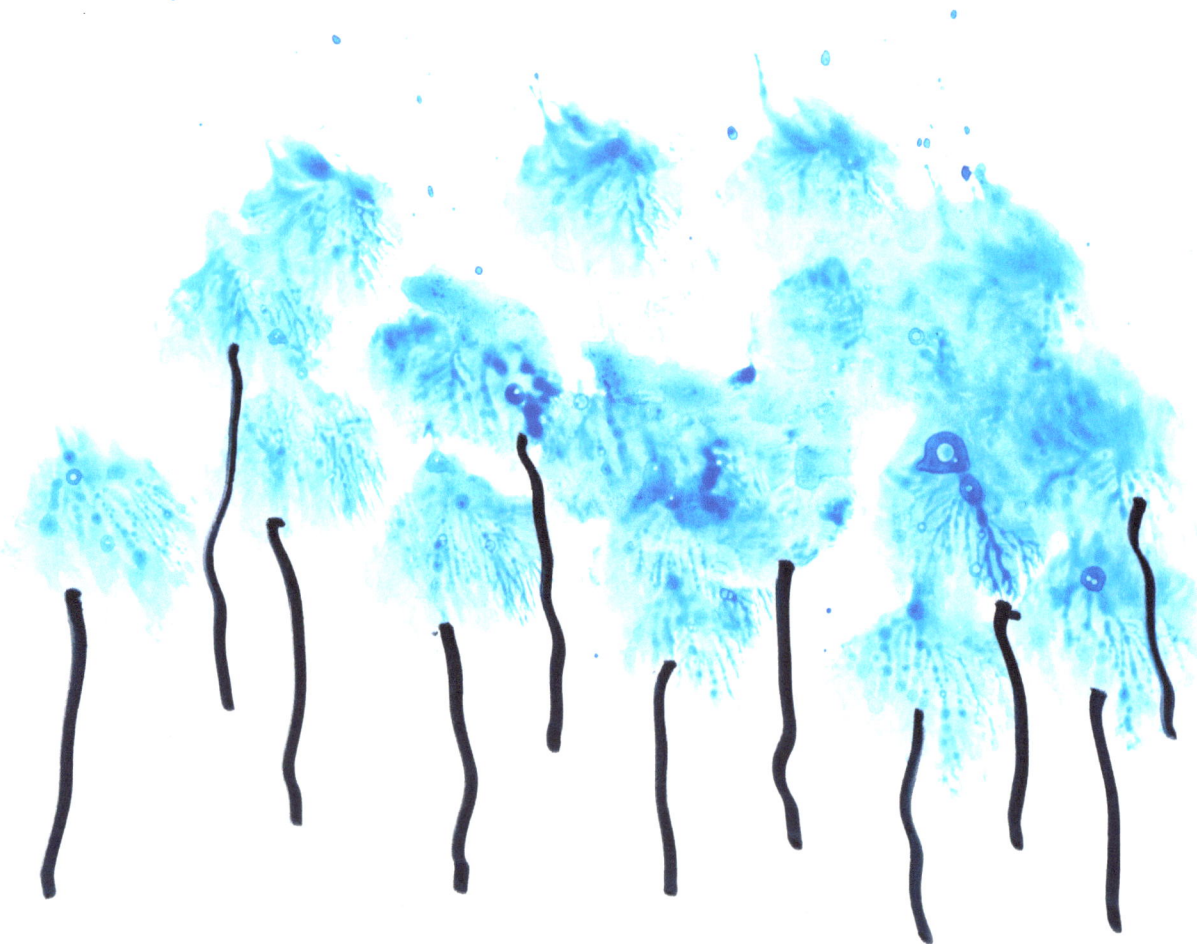

It doesn't matter which chakra we are in; we will still have the mind. We go to school, we learn the ABCs, we learn how to drive, we learn how to cook. We have developed the mind, and it is almost always there. Only in the seventh chakra do we go beyond the mind, but in the other six, we are always using the mind. Even in the seventh chakra, you can still use the mind. So the mind is a common ground for all the chakras. Dogs don't have a mind. They are totally instinctual. They go with instinct. Humans have instinct and mind. So yes, the mind is always there with you.

In the second chakra, when the ego comes up, the emotional body gets involved. The emotions in this body are very raw and sensitive. The smallest thing can bother them. Once these raw emotions are triggered, the emotional body, using the mind, pulls up old negative memories, and we perceive everything through this negativity. When this happens, the emotional body has taken over the mind.

The emotional body has no logic in it. It cannot think and be rational. It can only feel the memories of the negative past. The emotional body takes an emotional memory from ten years ago and cannot separate this old memory from new memories or experiences from today. It combines these two memories and creates a new story that isn't true, logically or sequentially. For example, the emotional body says, "When you were talking to me, you were looking at the wall. That means you hate me." It has come up with a story that is not accurate. We call this illusion. In these illusions, we always get hurt because the emotional body only holds on to negative emotions. To remain centered when we tune into the second chakra, we need to move into the higher chakras. We need to move to the fourth, fifth, sixth, or seventh chakra. With this centeredness we look at the light side of life, not the heavy side. We call this playfulness.

We fall apart because underneath we are sad. We get angry and upset but underneath this is sadness. Sadness is female and relates to the second chakra, to the emotional body. Sadness is the base or the bottom of the emotional body. It is the floor we sit on. So the second chakra is connected to sadness.

When we feel negative about something or something comes up that we don't like, we fall apart. When we fall apart, the energy may initially go to the third chakra, which is more male, and we will get angry and upset. We get fed up. Sometimes the energy will sit in the third chakra for a bit, but because of its heaviness, it will fall back down to the second chakra, and if we go to our emotional body, we feel sad. Sadness is the ground or the soil for the soul to become a human being. It is interesting that this planet *is* a planet of sadness. Now, when you ask me why am I sad, my answer could be because you are alive on this planet of sadness. In fact, it is a miracle not to be sad here. So now we know if we are sad, it is because we are alive.

Now we know why we are sad, but what do we do about this sadness. In our lives, we create situations with people close to us that trigger sadness to come to the surface. It comes to the surface so we can experience sadness to the point where we become total with it. Anytime we are total with something, it no longer bothers us. If we get bothered by sadness, it shows that we are still half-n-half, we have not become total in our experiencing yet. What I mean is, half of us is experiencing sadness while the other half hates it. Being total means not disliking or fighting our experiences. We experience our sadness without thinking it is bad or wanting to get rid of it. When we get total with sadness, all of a sudden the center of the energy of sadness opens up and at the center of sadness is happiness. We become happy.

So how to not be sad? When you are sad, don't dislike it. Say to yourself, "this is wonderful." When we really mean it, instantly the sadness breaks down and its center, which is happiness, comes out. We become happy. This is a dual world. There is positivity and negativity, happiness and sadness and both sides are fine. When we accept anything, then that thing is fine. Sadness is fine. When we know this, sadness breaks down and disappears. It may come back tomorrow. If it does, we will do the same thing again. We will accept sadness every day. Soon we will be able to transform sadness right away. So tell yourself, "sadness is fine, I like it." Then you are not split in two anymore. Usually there is one part sadness and one part not liking the sadness. With this split we cannot be total, we lose energy. Then we don't have the energy to go inside, break the sadness open and reach happiness. This is fantastic.

If we are in our heart, we are open. But when someone criticizes us, we close ourselves and fall into the second chakra or the emotional body. In the emotional body there is a lot of negative energy, and we feel it. From there, we either go one step higher to the third chakra, where negativity becomes anger, or we go one step lower to the first chakra, where negativity becomes repression and passivity. With passivity, you become sad.

When we express ourselves, we are no longer passive. Then we will not be aggressive either. The law of duality says if we are passive, we will be aggressive and vice versa, but when we are neither, we go beyond duality to assertiveness. When we express more and more, we move beyond this pattern of passive/aggressiveness. Things will not build up in us. When we are assertive, we are gentle, then we express our feelings more because when we are gentle, we don't hurt other people. We learn gradually that with this gentleness, we can say everything and nobody gets hurt.

When we are angry and express it to others, others get angry back, so we learn to become passive/aggressive. Out of fear of retaliation, we become passive. We try not to say things when we don't like something or are hurt, but at one point it gets to be too much, and we lash out. We are aggressive. With passive/aggressiveness, we will always have problems with others.

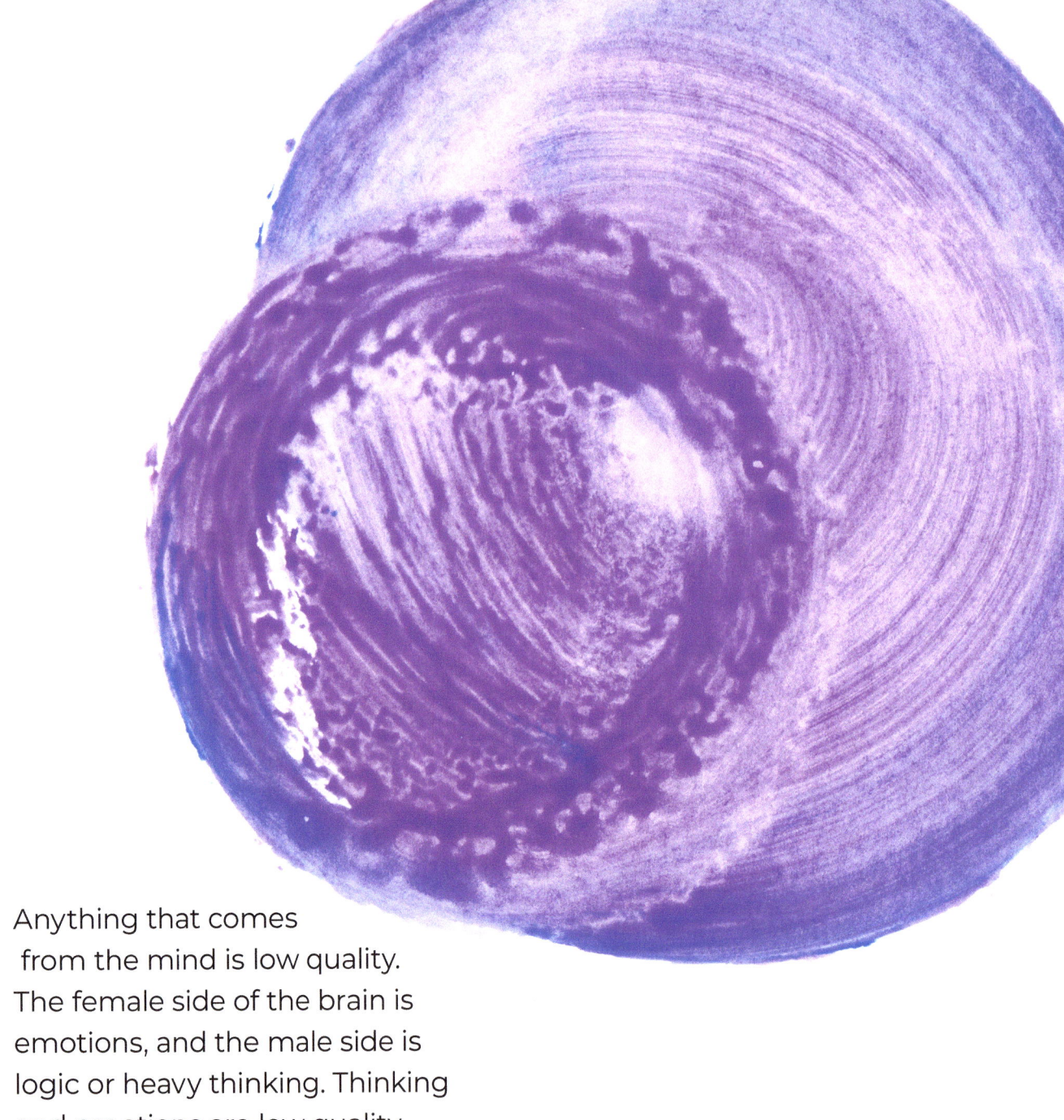

Anything that comes from the mind is low quality. The female side of the brain is emotions, and the male side is logic or heavy thinking. Thinking and emotions are low quality compared to compassion.

If we don't control, we think we are weak. When we are this flimsy or lacking in self-confidence, we are definitely in the lower self. The lower self constantly controls because it doesn't want to be weak, but needing to control is itself so weak. It shows the weakness of the lower self. The lower self thinks, "If I don't control, if things don't go according to what I want, then the situation is out of my hands, and I am weak." It is very interesting that the lower self gets everything wrong.

The female is pragmatic. When something doesn't make sense, she doesn't do it. It doesn't mean that she is lazy. If she sees something doesn't make sense, she recognizes it and she doesn't do it. The male doesn't have that quality because the mind doesn't have it. The mind goes with its programming. Whatever program is in the mind, it follows, just like a machine. But the female has intuition which means she has a connection with the soul, and that is why she is pragmatic. Remember, every human being has both the male and the female within them.

When we think, "I am doing great, no one else can do this the way I do," we feel a sense of pride, and that leads to feeling superior. In Existence, nothing is higher or lower than anything else. This "higher or lower than" is a function of the mind and therefore is illusory.

If I make life hard for myself, I will make it hard for others also. We are all one, so however we treat ourselves, we treat others. The only thing that separates us is our mind, which is totally conditioned by society, and the mind is not the real us.

When we say, "I knew this would happen, but I was hoping it wouldn't," of course it will happen, because knowing is much stronger than hoping. Hoping is just lala-land. So if you know something but you hope otherwise, just know that the known will happen, because knowing is always stronger than hoping.

Question: Why does it feel like I never get what I want, but everyone else gets everything they want?

When we worry so much about getting things we want, it has the opposite or reverse effect. So with worry, we don't get what we want. If others get everything they want, it is because they're not worried about it. If they want something, it happens. So worrying has the reverse effect. If we want something badly and we worry about it, it won't happen. Or if we don't want something badly and we worry about it, it will happen. For sure it will happen. It's just the reverse effect of worrying. Worrying is negativity, and negativity, intense negativity, always pushes away what we want. If we are positive, our positivity attracts what we want.

There is a rule in Existence that says if a person is cheap, Existence will be cheap towards them. If a person is generous, Existence will be generous back. That's the rule. The only person who can break this rule is an enlightened person. Everyone else will be cheap with a cheap person. An enlightened person can break this rule, because the enlightened person is aware of the problem, can express themselves, and therefore, can help the person to understand their cheapness. Of course, the enlightened person will not break the rules for people who can't or don't want to understand. Existence really shows us who we are. It is a reflection of who we are now. Because the enlightened person is generous, the cheap person will be attracted to this generosity. With this attraction, they will often open themselves and with this openness the enlightened person can work with them. By being generous to a cheap person, the enlightened person helps bring deeper reasons as to why this individual is cheap and helps them to grow beyond it.

If I criticize and laugh at people, no problem; if someone does that same thing to me, I hate it. If I never put anyone down, then if someone puts me down or laughs at me, I will laugh with them. I will be okay with it. It will not bother me. Overall, if I am harsh with people, I am afraid of others because I am afraid they will be harsh with me. We always look at people through our own experiences.

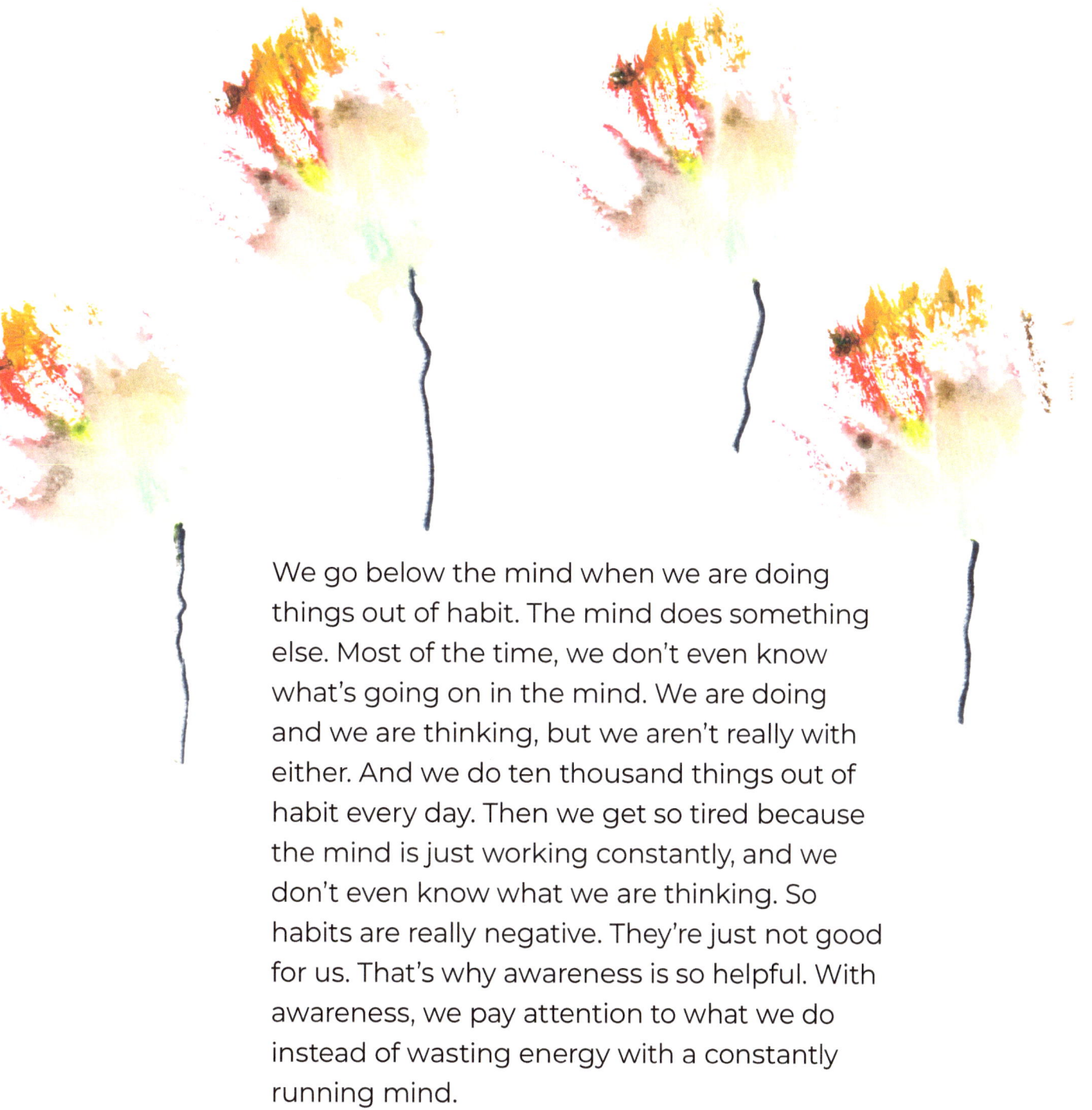

We go below the mind when we are doing things out of habit. The mind does something else. Most of the time, we don't even know what's going on in the mind. We are doing and we are thinking, but we aren't really with either. And we do ten thousand things out of habit every day. Then we get so tired because the mind is just working constantly, and we don't even know what we are thinking. So habits are really negative. They're just not good for us. That's why awareness is so helpful. With awareness, we pay attention to what we do instead of wasting energy with a constantly running mind.

The mind is always busy. It is always trying to figure something out or worrying about something. So the mind is constantly active. If it gets quiet, things become clear, and with clarity understanding happens. With understanding, we experience a real feeling of peacefulness. We call this feeling love. Love means inner peace. Often understanding clears up a lot of the misunderstandings that come from society or our culture, that create hardship and hell for us. Most of these conditionings are a thousand years old.

So love means inner peace. Awareness means being clear, or clarity. When the mind becomes clear, it gives us joy. It feels so good, and that joyfulness is love.

If deep inside we feel that we are not worthy, the mind creates many scenarios and stories to prove to us that we are not worthy. And we believe these stories. "Nobody wants me, nobody wants to be with me." These are all the creation of the mind. From this deep wound of feeling not worthy, we constantly reflect energy out to others that suggests we are not worthy. What we need to know is that in the universe there is love and everybody is equal. But we create our life according to the emotional wounds that we have. We separate ourselves from others because we are protecting ourselves. In this way, there is always this separation. All of this is purely the thoughts and imagination of the mind. The mind itself is the problem. In any situation, if we bring the mind in, we mess up the situation. We blow it out of proportion. We either see ourselves as the best or as the worst— the mind constantly goes to extremes. The mind is unsettling and makes us unsettled.

When we become aware of some negativity that we have been hiding in the unconscious, it becomes conscious. Then we can see and understand it. So understanding comes with awareness. Awareness happens in many ways. It can happen with meditation. It also happens when you feel open, totally open. Openness means love. So when you really feel love, you become aware. You become so sensitive; you sense things. You are alive. So all these, love, awareness, and meditation, are one thing when we go deeper. On the surface, they seem different. I meditate but I'm not loving. Or I love someone, but I don't meditate. No, no, no. When you love someone, you are meditating. When you're meditating and you really open yourself, then you're loving. If you keep meditating and you're not loving, that just shows that your meditation is not working yet. It is not going deeper. You are sitting, but still the mind is running. We might not even notice the mind running because meditation has become a habit. Habits are almost like dreams. With habit, it is as if we are sleeping or dreaming, but we are not aware of our dreams. The mind is running but we are not aware of it. The mind works or thinks even when we sleep, the mind works because you have dreams, but you're not even aware of it.

When we have any conflict, it is because of problems we've had since we were born coming to the surface from our memory banks. This causes turmoil, restlessness, and conflicts with others. Conflicts in a relationship lead to fighting and bickering, which can make us feel guilty and/or belittled afterwards. And conflicts are not only with others. We have lots of conflicts inside too. This turmoil is constantly going on in our subconscious.

Over time, these conflicts become a habit that we are not even aware of. If we become aware that we are trying to disagree with someone from our past by disagreeing with someone else now, we can stop it immediately. We have the freedom to stop it now, because we are looking at the roots of the problem. So the only way to get out of these habitual conflicts is to become more aware. With awareness, the turmoil will automatically go away. We become free of it. There is magic in awareness.

So all we have to do is to become more aware. Awareness happens through understanding, meditation, love, which bring unity with others, and becoming one hundred percent present in the moment. Laughter and crying also make us more aware because they bring us to the moment. Overall, if we live totally, our awareness grows because we come to the moment. The more aware we become, the less inner conflict and heaviness there will be in us. We become lighter and lighter.

When we act from habit, we are not aware. But when we look and see something more clearly, we act from awareness.

When we have a goal, we become limited by that goal. Everything else goes out of our sight; we are focused on our goal. We are not open to the bigger picture, or what life wants to give us. We tell ourselves we will become happy when we reach our goal, but as soon as we reach one goal, we create another. In this way, we are always deferring happiness. I am not saying don't have goals. I am saying be happy while you are attending to your goals. With happiness, we are open and flexible.

When we are ashamed of something, we really want to hide that thing. We either keep it locked away in the unconscious or, if we are conscious of it, we don't show or express it, we keep it hidden. But when we hide, we never get to look more deeply into that thing. We never allow it to come up, we never open it to understand it. Understanding deeply resolves the problem. So if you have a connection with an enlightened person, please don't be ashamed of anything, because then you will get help. That thing will be resolved. It will become healthy. It is only when we hide something that it becomes unhealthy, and hiding affects our whole life, our body, everything, in a negative way. Please, if you're ashamed of something, try to understand it. Understanding is so powerful. Never ever censor yourself with a guide on a spiritual path. You will feel so relaxed, so let go. Compassion and understanding together are a powerful tool. Compassion comes from the heart and understanding comes from the fifth chakra. With the heart chakra and the fifth chakra (with compassion and understanding), we can solve any problem.

The reason people complain about their job is because they really don't like their job, but they do it anyway. In this way, they are repressing. But if you love something and you do it with totality, you never complain. Complaining means we don't want to do what we are doing. It's possible that your conscious wants to do it, but your unconscious doesn't like it. Then there's an inner conflict and complaining is the result.

There are three stages we must pass through in the lower self before we can move to the higher self. In the first stage, we are not aware of subtleties around us at all. In the second stage, we become aware of only negativities and because of this limited awareness, we are constantly in trouble with others. We start abusing others. In the third stage, we see the negativity of others and still have a lot of judgment, but we don't get involved. We see it, but we keep it to ourselves. These are all stages of the lower self. But when we become aware of our judgment of others' negativity and our abuse of others, this awareness gets rid of the negativity in us. Then we move to the next stage: to the higher self. Here we can see the negativity of others, but it does not bother us at all. We even find positivity in the negativity.

When we become angry, we lose our power. We might think we become more powerful, but it is a negative power, and negative power cannot create anything positive. However, if we stay centered, not only what we want but also what we say becomes effective, and we succeed.

Power is in being subtle. People who are harsh are weak. They fight with others, but deep inside they think they are not good enough and others are not good either. When you are subtle and gentle, you like others and deep down you like yourself. This gives you power. Power comes with subtlety and gentleness.

Anything that is negative creates fear and fear makes everything a big deal. So we make a big deal out of anything negative.

Thinking about the future closes our heart because there is so much uncertainty in the future. This uncertainty triggers fear and fear closes the heart. Being in the present opens the heart. The past doesn't involve the heart either. It has to do with the lower chakras. So with the unknown or the future, there is fear. There could be a small amount of excitement about the possibilities the future might hold, but mostly there is fear. Because the past is known, there is no fear in it and no possibilities either. We cannot change the past. There is no excitement or joy either. That's why the past doesn't involve the heart. The past is dead.

God has many different parts. There is the language part of God and the feeling part of God. Getting in touch with the language of God is called getting in touch with the truth. When we get in touch with the feeling part of God, we experience bliss. The interesting thing is, if we get in touch with one of these, we will be connected to both. So if we are blissful, we have the capacity to understand the truth, and when we understand the truth, we feel blissful. Understanding involves the mind and the soul. Bliss involves only the soul.

Often we fall into the energy of others. Let's look at how this happens. Our thinking mostly comes from what we learned from childhood up to now, all of which is the past and comes from others. When we are in our minds, we have fallen into something that doesn't exist anymore, something that is dead. For example, all our conditionings are from other people who got them from other people who got them from society. All the shoulds and should nots are from society. None of these are us, they are the lower self. We are pure bliss. If, instead of falling into the energy of our surroundings, we could fall into the energy of our soul, every minute would be fresh and blissful. The freshness of the moment has so many advantages. We feel so much love and with this love comes a subtle, beautiful wisdom that helps us to mature. When we are mature, we are on target and having fun!

Mind collects wounds from the past. Then anytime we look at life with the mind, we see it through our wounds and many things look negative. When we see ourselves through these wounds, we think, "Oh, I am not good enough." We look at others and think, "Oh, this person is so stupid." We look at a job that needs doing, and we think it's hard or useless. So mostly the mind sees the negative. Then we don't feel good and over time we become cynical, and we can't trust. If someone says you are good or you are beautiful, we think they don't mean it, even though in our mind we have a desire to be the best. Then we start being afraid of people who like us. We call this a fear of love.

    This fear will damage any relationship gradually, which only proves or reinforces our belief that love is scary and not to be trusted. So every time we fall in love, deep inside we have a fear of it, which again will damage any new relationship. I know many people who, if you express to them that you like them, they get frightened or they don't believe it—they have become cynical, because they are looking through the negativity of their inner wounds.

When we identify with someone, we get all their negativity and heaviness. It transfers to us. So just in that identification, we get all their negativity. And everybody has some negativity, so identifying is detrimental to us. It is no good.

If there was no space for us to open ourselves and express our feelings as a child, if there was always a dictatorship at home from parents or outside the home from society, then we cannot express ourselves now. Instead, as we grow older, when we get angry, we become dictators ourselves. If we were given space to express ourselves as children, then when we grow up, we will be able to express ourselves, and we will almost never need to get angry. Sometimes we will, but most of the time we won't. We will be freer in life overall.

A boy inside the mother's womb starts kicking and when he comes out, he is noisy and has a lot of energy. A girl is soft and plays with dolls. The boy runs around and kicks the walls and is always in a sense in trouble. He is always told to be quiet, and not to destroy things—don't do this, don't do that, don't, don't, don't. And, because of that, his emotions become repressed. That is why it is harder for a man to express himself. In a relationship, they often create trouble, because of this repression. Even in relationship with themselves, they have problems, inner struggles and conflict. In this way, their whole life becomes very messy.

We worry about and want to be considerate of others, because from childhood we have been told to be considerate of them. But this consideration should be in moderation. Moderation means we shouldn't do something too much nor should we avoid it altogether. If we don't consider others at all, we become cruel, and if we worry about people too much our connection with them becomes ineffective. It will damage the connection. It will damage the friendship. We become a mother to them, a worried mother.

Many women do not want sex, but because they have a partner, they get forced into it. Then they start resenting their partner. There are many reasons why men and women fight, like finances or jealousy, but sex is one of the biggest. The woman does not like the partner unconsciously because of this issue, and it creates a lot of problems.

When we take things personally, there is so much illusion involved. It is the ego that takes things personally, and the ego itself is all illusion. We should always check with others to see if they are actually talking about us or bothered by us. If they say yes, that just means we have some issues we need to work on. Only the ego gets offended. This situation is a great opportunity for us to focus on an issue and work on it. The ego thinks it has to be perfect. We just need to understand the ego is not us. It has hangups and problems. Our job is to bring understanding to its problems, because understanding solves all problems. Remember, getting offended only happens to the ego, not us and it has become a habit.

Wanting to be cared for means we want others to care for us and that is very harsh. We don't consider people and who they are. They have to care for us or we don't care for them. It is so selfish to expect others to care for us. If we just accept people the way they are, they feel so relaxed that they start caring for us. That is how the universe works.

If we take things seriously, we are ready to get bothered. The universe is not serious. Reality is not serious; it is very playful. We are much more intense about the affairs of the universe than the universe itself. In a sense, we want to be better than the universe. The universe is so playful and flexible. In seriousness, there is no flexibility and because of that, we often fall apart. When we are serious, we are not flexible. We are ready to fall apart if things do not go our way, or if there is even a hint that things may not go our way. We feel bad. It doesn't matter what happens really, when we are serious, every moment we are ready to fall apart and be miserable. Flexibility is the highest standard. It is living at the level of reality, of God or Existence.

When we cry, we feel bad because we go with our conditioning that says crying is bad. The mind comes in and says, "Crying is stupid. You are stupid. Don't cry. It is childish." These are the destructive voices of the mind. But crying is wonderful; it is a let go of heaviness. Crying is beautiful. Laughter is also beautiful. They both help us get rid of heaviness.

When we think something is bad, we feel bad because we are taking that thing seriously. If we think it's not bad, then it's okay, and we don't take it seriously. When we bring acceptance to anything, it becomes healthy and playful. When we are playful, we take a softer and gentler approach to things, and we feel more confidence.

The earth is all about growth. To stay alive, we need to have some issues, because, if we don't have any problems, we will not grow.

Without the imprints of old childhood traumas, there would be no planet earth. So if planet Earth exists, it is because of those childhood traumas. Without them, there is no point for us to be here. They help us along the way to grow, so they are absolutely necessary.

This whole game of being on Earth is for Existence to grow. The animals and trees all evolve and become human beings and then become God. We grow when we encounter negativity and understand what that negativity means for us. If someone hates us or is angry with us, we need to understand this negativity more deeply. It is an opportunity for us to grow.

Another example of negativity is when we think too much or worry. Worry, fear, or hatred create dark energy, which we call karma. Every time we create karma, somebody has to show up to help us get rid of that karma by mistreating us. This is one way. Another way is to use breathing exercises to clean negative energy or karma. But the best way is not to create karma in the first place by being more gentle, softer and more subtle.

If we think Existence is anything but pure love, we are wrong. Everything in Existence is pure love. When we think this way, we start trusting Existence. If someone talks behind someone else's back, that is what Existence wants; what is wrong with that? This is what we call trust, but the mind constantly goes back to what we have learned from society. Society says, "These people are horrible and nasty, and how dare they treat us like this." When we understand that Existence is all love, society's views don't apply anymore. Then we can love and with that comes deep relaxation, which leads to us trusting more and more.

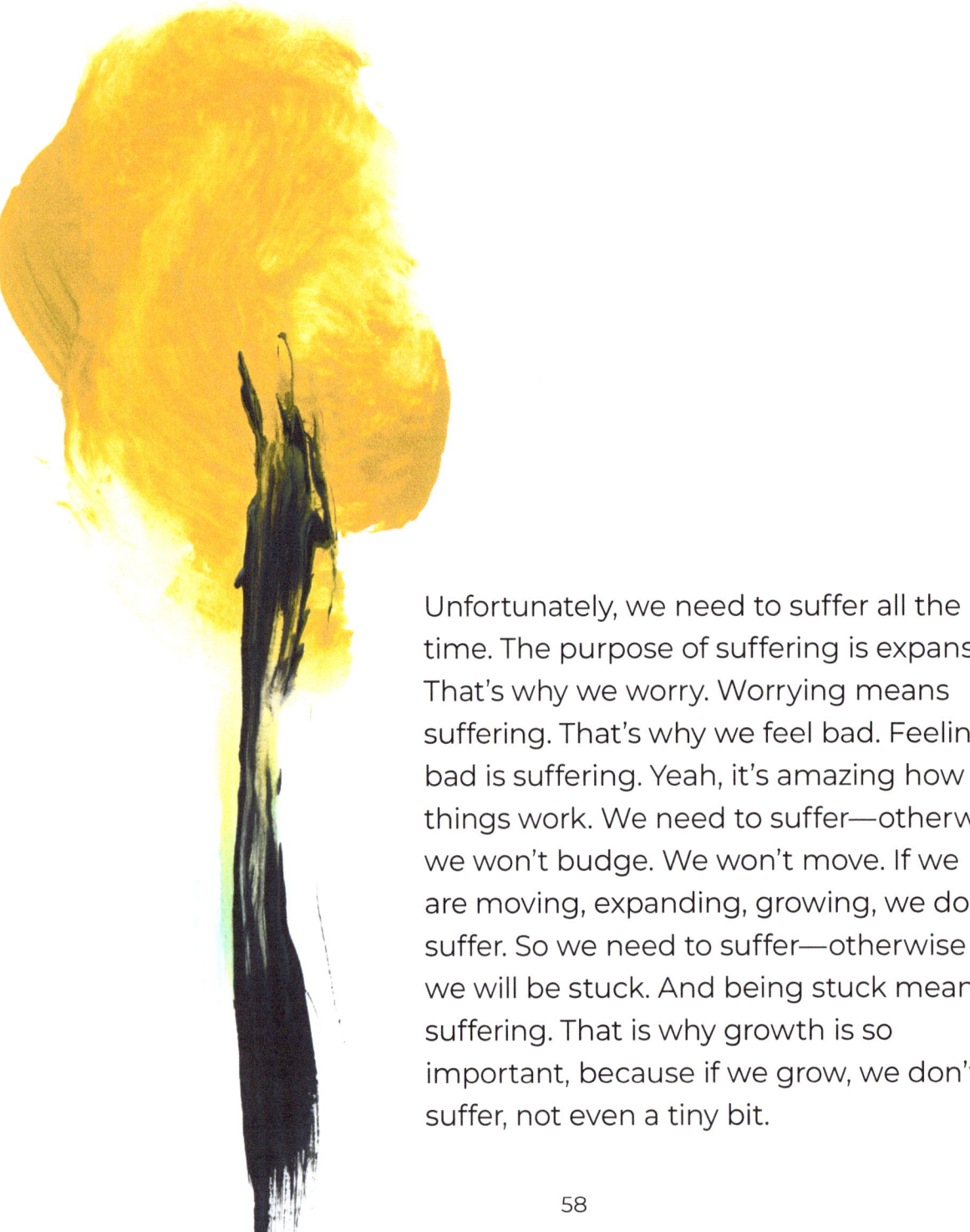

Unfortunately, we need to suffer all the time. The purpose of suffering is expansion. That's why we worry. Worrying means suffering. That's why we feel bad. Feeling bad is suffering. Yeah, it's amazing how things work. We need to suffer—otherwise we won't budge. We won't move. If we are moving, expanding, growing, we don't suffer. So we need to suffer—otherwise we will be stuck. And being stuck means suffering. That is why growth is so important, because if we grow, we don't suffer, not even a tiny bit.

In life, Existence favors us with incidents to take away karma that we made by hurting ourselves or others. Usually, these incidents are uncomfortable. For example, someone yells at us unjustly or mistreats us, but in doing so they take away a lot of our karma. If we don't understand what Existence is doing when these incidents happen, we resist or fight back and replace the karma that was taken with new karma. By not trusting Existence, we lose an opportunity to cleanse ourselves. But even if we miss this chance to grow, Existence will continue to try to help by creating more problems for us. For example, someone might talk behind our back or mistreat us. When this happens, it is uncomfortable, but if we remember that Existence is only trying to take our karma away, we not only cleanse karma, but over time, we will gain trust and a deeper understanding that Existence is all love. We live in a dual world. Existence works with us according to this duality to bring balance and growth. It seems complex, but it really is very simple.

Everyone has their own special experiences in life. Experiences that are unique to them and tailored for their growth. Growth means moving towards negative energy and then coming back to the positive again. Each time we do this, the positive expands a little bit. So we expand our positive side by going to the negative side. That is why an authentic person is never afraid of the negative, because it helps them to expand more.

When our understanding increases, we don't need a lot of pressure to grow or expand. Existence doesn't need to give us accidents and sickness and problems to motivate us. But, when our understanding is not enough, we need problems and pressures so we can bring understanding to them, which leads to growth.

One rule of Existence is that the only time we get pushed by others is when we resist. If we don't resist, then others cannot be pushy.

Only when we worry and are concerned do problems arise. When there is no concern in us and we are at ease, problems disappear. There will be no problems. Problems only exist because we worry about something.

If we hurt someone unintentionally, which means our unconscious is hurting them, somehow that must have been necessary for them. Otherwise, it wouldn't have happened. That person needed to get hurt so they could grow. How else can God help them grow? When it's no longer necessary, it won't happen anymore. If it is happening, it is absolutely needed. We just have to trust Existence in every moment and in every circumstance. It is important to understand that this only applies to unintentionally hurting someone. If we hurt someone intentionally, our ego gets involved. It wants to punish or discipline others. God or Existence is not a mother who wants to discipline a child, God is only interested in our growth and our eventual freedom.

The universe is all about expansion. The whole universe, not only this planet. How do we expand? We expand when we are relaxed. With relaxation we enjoy, then we grow. So enjoyment helps us grow. How does enjoyment help us grow? When we enjoy, we are loving what we are doing. Then that doing becomes meditation. This expands our soul by reducing hurtful and negative energies in the mind and body and other deeper layers within us, like the etheric, mental, and emotional bodies. So growth means enjoyment. That's why everybody likes to enjoy. But if we don't do anything to expand, we suffer. Suffering means getting stuck, we don't move. Basically, we're in hell. If we move, if we grow and expand, we go to heaven. If we stop, if we don't grow, we're in hell. If we resist or hide or don't want to look at ourselves, we are miserable.

When you want something but you feel wanting that thing is wrong, you feel guilty. When you feel guilty, you don't value yourself anymore. When you don't value yourself, you do everything except those things that really take care of you. For example, let's say you have been conditioned that you shouldn't want more. Then when you want something, you might only think about it or you might even get it, but either way, deep inside, you feel guilty. When anyone feels guilty, they feel worthless and not good enough. Then, because you feel worthless, you don't attend to the wellbeing of your body, emotions and/or thoughts. You don't care what you feel or what you think. This is repression.

     When we repress, it's because we think somehow we are doing something wrong. But we are not doing anything wrong. We have just been conditioned that this thing is wrong. It could be any kind of conditioning. We have to look into our lives and see what we think is wrong. We need to understand that many things we were taught from childhood are foolish, and that when we feel guilty about something we have thought or done, we will also neglect something we have been taught is important. It could be our body, or our emotions, our home…. We just have to pay attention to where we have a limiting conditioning, so we can free ourselves.

Disliking or not accepting is an ego attribute. Acceptance is an element of the divine within us. Ego is the lower part of us and acceptance is the higher part. When we accept, our soul runs our life, or when our soul runs our life, we accept. They basically happen simultaneously. So anytime we don't accept something, our ego is in charge. When this happens, our soul rests, so we don't get the benefit of its energy. For example, if other people are fighting, our ego often gets involved and we get upset. Our soul, on the other hand, accepts this fighting and gives space to it. Our higher self knows that life is not possible without problems.

Existence creates all negativity. Our only job is to accept the negativity and not get upset. Acceptance is the key. Existence has created everything for a higher reason. All we need to do is to have acceptance for what Existence has created.

If we do something that makes us feel good about ourselves, like deeply understanding something, we become closer to ourselves and others. If we do something that we don't like, then we dislike ourselves, we feel funny and we separate from others. With dislike, the mind starts finding faults and problems with others. People around us are the same all the time, but when we don't feel good about ourselves, we become more sensitive to the negativity of others and start thinking they have something against us. When we feel good about ourselves, others can be negative, and we won't take it personally. So feeling good about the self takes the ego out of the picture, and without the ego we don't take things personally.

We can categorize people into three types for the sake of simplicity: primitive, normal, and advanced. In the first stage, one doesn't have enough intelligence or awareness to understand what society demands of them, so they live primitively. They don't care what society thinks of them or how they look. In the second stage, one gets influenced by society. They have the desire to fit into society, so they really care about how society sees them. The third stage happens when we have grown and become more subtle. Then the opinion of society has no influence over us, because it is not important to us anymore. We are totally aware of what society wants from us, but we are above it. We might decide to look good or not, but we really don't care about the opinion of society. We only care about the opinion of society when we don't accept ourselves. Instead, we want society to accept us. If we accept ourselves, then society has no hold on us.

Humans are divided into two types, people who do not accept themselves and those who do not accept others. Of course, there are those who are a mix of these two, but most people are of the first category. If we don't accept ourselves, it is because in the past, other people put us down—maybe our mom, dad, or teachers. Somebody has put us down and now we think we are not good enough, and we do not accept ourselves.

When we start to bring a deeper understanding to ourselves and our issues, we begin to accept ourselves more. The ego gets pushed aside with acceptance and becomes big with rejection. Without any understanding of the self, our ego feels that it is better than others. The ego needs to put other people down because it doesn't have any substance itself. It feels empty and fake inside. When we accept ourselves without understanding, the ego could use it to get big. It could get lost in how great we are. But if we accept ourselves with deeper understanding, the ego doesn't get big. Understanding is the anti-ego!

One reason we feel depressed is because we think we are not where we are supposed to be. But the fact is we are exactly where we are supposed to be. The mind comes in and says, "I should be better. I should be more advanced." Then we are caught in a catch-22. This worry causes us to be tense. But if we accept who and where we are, then we are relaxed, and relaxation is exactly where we are supposed to be. Deep relaxation is meditation. And in this state, we feel an openness which brings love for others. But when we start worrying, we are not relaxed anymore. The mind creates disturbance, and we become depressed. This is all the craziness of the mind. But nothing is wasted in Existence, even worrying and tension, because any suffering will push us toward growth.

Ego means living in illusions. The world we live in, or the illusional world we live in, is seen through our training and conditioning. It is perceived according to our experiences and upbringing. So according to our conditioning and upbringing, we make up stories in our head about what we are experiencing. And everybody's story of life is different, so everyone creates a different kind of illusion out of their experience, which is different than other people having the same experience.

Ego always thinks of other people as less than. Other people's egos think the same. Ego, in general, thinks everybody else is less than. They are below us.

Humans have both an inferiority and a superiority complex. If we have one in the conscious mind, then we have the other in the unconscious mind. That is why sometimes we feel inferior and sometimes we feel superior. When we compare ourselves with others, we either feel superior or inferior to them. So comparison either brings out our unconscious mind, or it emphasizes the conscious mind. Either way, it is a tool used by the ego to make us feel better than or worse than others.

Let's say you are unaware of how on top of things you are. You have strong willpower, but you don't know it. You think you are weak. What does that mean? Basically, it means the ego has not recognized that you have a strong will, that you are strong. This is wonderful! Then I tell you you are very strong, and I show you examples of your strong points. Because you learn this within the parameters of understanding, it goes deeper into your soul. Your mind doesn't grasp it. Because of this, the mind or the ego will not start feeling proud. It is just some information you know about yourself. If you knew it already, without understanding, you would be so proud. You would have a big ego, and with a big ego, you wouldn't want to understand anything about yourself. "What do I need to understand? I am perfect." With a big ego, we are really lost.

    If we are open to understanding, our ego is not the boss, it is not in charge. We are open and with this openness, we can see how much the ego is running the show and how much our higher self is running the show. This is very subtle.

We want to talk about the uniqueness of the love of Existence. Existence loves everyone. There is nothing unique about it. But every single person is different. Every person is unique. So when Existence loves someone, it does so on their level, based on their unique personality and being. Existence's love is the same for everyone, but its expression is very unique. It's not general. It is very special because it's unique for each person.

When somebody judges us, and we feel put down, something happens. Because society doesn't know about the duality of Existence, it teaches us that being put down is bad, and bad is terrible. So society says nobody should judge you or put you down. Then, because we don't know the higher either, because we only know what society teaches us, we fall apart when we are judged. We don't like to be judged or put down. But Existence is not society. Society is just a child.

The reality of Existence is that if someone puts us down, somewhere else, because Existence is so fair, something will happen to bring us up. These two balance each other. Conversely, if someone builds us up, then somewhere else, soon, we will need to go down. These two always go together. So just remember that if someone judges you or laughs at you, in the very near future, something great is going to happen, or something negative that was going to happen won't happen. And we will never know what that negative thing might have been. There could be an accident that was going to happen that now won't happen because somebody put you down. So you see, even though we might not be able to tell what is what, we have to know that if people put us down, or if they put us up, it doesn't matter. Anything that happens is fantastic. We just have to understand that we are dealing with the duality of Existence.

Seeing something negative in ourselves and being able to express it is very advanced. It shows that our awareness has grown enough to see ourselves. This planet is the planet of duality. When we see ourselves, we go beyond duality. Awareness takes us beyond duality, and we become one with Existence.

The ocean is both the drop and the ocean, and the drop is both the ocean and the drop. We are both the ocean and the drop.

Question: I don't get it. Here I am working on myself and growing, and I seem lower than everyone else around me.

When we are not ready to do inner work, our chakras remain clean. When we are ready to start our inner work, then our chakras become clogged and dirty so we can work on ourselves. These blockages are hindrances that need to be removed by growing. Cleaning our chakras makes our consciousness vaster. If a person is not ready to grow, there is no reason for them to have clogged chakras. They just continue to do their worldly life and are comfortable the way they are.

So don't compare yourself to others. No one is higher than anybody else. We are all one and Existence is all about love. Our body has billions of cells; together they make one body. How can they be separated? Humans are all cells of one body. They cannot be separated. How can one cell be better than any other one? Only the mind thinks in terms of better or worse.

If someone is shy, it is because in their childhood, they were mistreated by others. Now they feel better being alone than when they are with others. They are afraid of others. For these people, being alone is very healing. Meditation is a good path for them. In meditation, they connect to their soul and love happens. There are two ways to connect to the soul. It can either happen in meditation or in relating with another. A person's heart can become very open to another. That open heart becomes a door to the soul. When the heart is open, the energy of the soul comes out.

When a society is more advanced, the mind becomes more developed than the heart, and when that happens people become distant from each other. Intellectual people are shy and want to stay away from others, so their path is meditation. In the old days, the West was undeveloped. That is why religions that were born in the West don't stress meditation—they focus on love. The East was advanced, so religions born in the East were based on meditation.

There are two paths: the path of meditation and the path of love. For many people, they both apply. Being on both paths is a very refined state and can be hard. You want to meditate, but the path of love comes in and you can't meditate. Then you miss meditation, so again you meditate for a while, which causes your love to grow, and then again you don't meditate. These people have both a strong male and a strong female. This is very advanced. So if you are on both paths and you are not meditating, it's okay. Stick with deeper understanding, which is a common factor of both love and meditation. Understanding is right in the middle, and without it we can't advance. If sometimes you don't feel like meditating, focus on love and understanding. And if you feel like meditating, meditate.

When you have love and understanding together, they become meditation. And if you have understanding and meditation together, they become love. Between love and meditation is understanding. If you add understanding to either side, it becomes the other. With the three of them, the mind slows down and you feel great. You experience your soul. You feel alive and younger. It brings life to you.

When we are on the path of love, we totally trust that Existence will give us exactly what is necessary. It might be hardship, so we can grow, or it could be joy. Whatever it gives us, we totally trust Existence. When our path is meditation, we have to include our own planning and organization. The path of meditation is basically male, so the path of meditation includes male characteristics. The path of love is female. On the path of love, we just have to trust, and things will become rosy and beautiful.

If we want to benefit from divine things—like love, trust, and meditation—we are bringing in greed, and greed doesn't work with the divine. Then our meditation will not be effective, and our trust and love will not be real. We won't be able to meditate, love, or trust. The mind always wants to take advantage, but the heart never takes advantage. If we go after the divine with the mind, we will never attain it. Only with the heart can you attain divine.

When a person is not very capable or competent, they always brag about the things they have done. If they could go deeper, they would encounter their weakness and incompetence. Experiencing incompetence is the way to heal it, and when the incompetence is gone, they won't need to brag anymore. Then they will have much better relationships with others. People tend to dislike those who brag. They betray them or lie to them or even accuse them, just because of bragging.

By going deep into our weak points, we come out of them, and we won't need to brag anymore. Our life becomes easy and successful. We will have a high-quality life financially, emotionally, and spiritually.

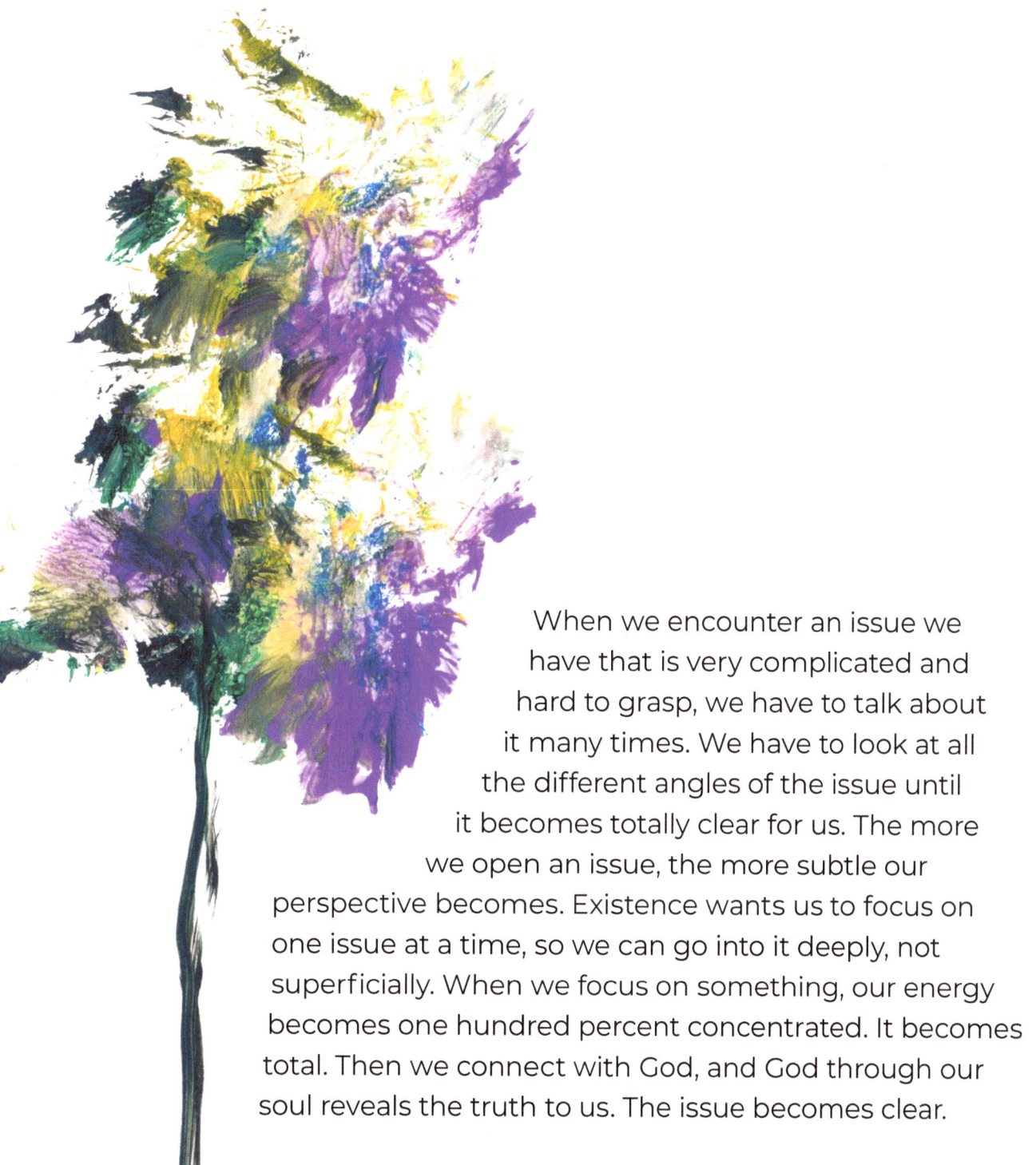

When we encounter an issue we have that is very complicated and hard to grasp, we have to talk about it many times. We have to look at all the different angles of the issue until it becomes totally clear for us. The more we open an issue, the more subtle our perspective becomes. Existence wants us to focus on one issue at a time, so we can go into it deeply, not superficially. When we focus on something, our energy becomes one hundred percent concentrated. It becomes total. Then we connect with God, and God through our soul reveals the truth to us. The issue becomes clear.

Something that comes from the mind cannot transform us, but something that comes from our depth can transform us.

Truth is eternal. Untruth creates suffering. So if we get disturbed by someone or something, it is the "untruth" in us, or the ego, that gets disturbed and falls apart. By looking deeper into the issue that created this disturbance, we can find the old emotional wound that has been triggered and uproot this wound. Negativities are opportunities. But usually when we get hurt, we either don't want to attend to the issue or even talk about it, or we fight with the person who pushed our button. Spirituality means using negativity as an opportunity to look at ourselves. So instead of fighting with others, we appreciate them for creating this hardship and giving us an opportunity to grow.

How can we get to eternal bliss from where we are? Whatever happens to us now is what we need to work on in this moment. Inner conflicts or outer conflicts and problems are there. When we look at them deeper, pay attention to them, and talk about them, understanding happens. When this happens, we experience our soul. We come out of our conditionings. We become satisfied and happy. Over time, the more this happens, the more we move from negativity and darkness to positivity and light. Then at one point, we will move to the light and stay there forever.

When we hear a mystical concept or understanding, the mind adds its own neuroses, expectations, fears, illusions, and anxieties to it. Then that understanding becomes a totally different concept, altered to fit with our neurosis, our deep inferiority complex, or whatever problems we have. So it's good to revisit our understanding of things, so we don't go with a wrong understanding for a long time. Also, Existence changes all the time; it becomes more advanced every day. Therefore, with today's understanding, we may have to let go of an older understanding. Always be prepared to throw old understandings away and be totally open and ready for any new understanding from Existence.

Understanding is a life-changing phenomenon. Really, when you understand something about yourself, your life changes. If something goes in one ear and we don't really get it, it is better that it keeps right on going out the other ear. But if it goes in and registers on our soul, we will never be the same. And when it registers on our soul, we understand something that is totally far out—it's beautiful, it's outstanding. When our soul grasps an understanding, it is chiseled or written into the soul, and we have it forever with us.

Humans experience two types of happiness. One is superficial because it involves the ego, and one is deep because the ego is not involved. Superficial happiness happens when people make fun of others or become happy because someone they don't like is experiencing misfortune. This happiness is superficial and annoying to others. But a deep happiness that comes from love and deep understanding makes everybody happy.

A person who is in a rush cannot see things deeply. They cannot understand deeply. They are always on the surface. If we want to see deeper and become total in anything, it cannot happen with rushing. Superficial things might get done with rushing, but if we want to work on ourselves, we should not rush.

When our level of anxiety reaches a certain point, we become destructive. Our minds are so consumed with this anxiety and worry that we are not present with what we are doing. We drop things, we bang things together and make too much noise in the kitchen. We become sloppy and destructive. And it's not just banging in the kitchen, anxiety creates banging within us too, causing physical problems and illness. The only thing in humans that becomes destructive is anxiety. For example, a tree doesn't have anxiety, and trees don't destroy things. Birds are the same. When there is no anxiety, nothing gets destroyed. If the world was only birds and animals, there would be no destruction. Only humans destroy because of so much anxiety in the mind and in the unconscious. We need to find a way to reduce anxiety with a deeper understanding of why we do what we do, and why we think what we think. With deeper understanding comes the right action.

Anger means our level of anxiety has gone beyond a certain point. From that point on, anxiety becomes anger.

When we do not accept ourselves, of course, we worry—and with worrying, there is no clarity. When there is no worrying, there is clarity. A clear mind never worries and therefore never suffers. If we accept ourselves with understanding, then there is clarity and with clarity, joy. But we also need clarity to understand. Actually, clarity is understanding. When things are clear to you, you understand. And when we understand, we say goodbye to any and all negativities—jealousy, anger, and what not.

Existence shows up for us according to how much credit we have with Existence. If I have a low bank account with Existence, for example, if I hurt people or cheat them, or treat them horribly, then everything becomes very low quality in my life. If I have a full bank account with Existence, then all the good things happen to me. Existence treats me according to my bank account. When we fully trust Existence, our bank account becomes full of positive energy. That trust gives us inner peace because we know everything is perfect. Even if we have a low bank account with Existence but we suddenly trust, immediately we start depositing into our inner account, and according to that everything becomes okay. Every time we trust, we deposit tons of positive energy into our inner bank account.

Success happens when we become total in whatever we do. When we are total, our inner energy or the energy of the soul gets involved. In any situation, work or otherwise, if you become total, you become successful—you feel satisfied and content. It brings a feeling of freedom to you.

How can we look at life as a delight? By trusting Existence. The more we trust Existence the more life becomes light and delightful.

There is a fine line between sympathy and compassion. When we are on the border of these two, we jump from one to the other and back again. If we stay on the side of compassion, we are in touch with our soul. The soul never feels bad or worries about anything. It knows that the oversoul is in charge and that everyone gets what they need for their growth in each moment. Because of this, there is nothing to worry about. If someone falls apart, it is because that person needs to learn and understand something. Everybody is living their purpose in life. Everyone is growing in some way. A mystic is someone who understands this deeply.

    If we want to stay in compassion, we have to trust Existence. Even if the worst thing happens to us or to our loved ones, we still trust that this is happening for that person's wellbeing. We are like a wave in the ocean that is created by the wind. The wind is our breath. Although the wave looks separate from the ocean, it is part of the ocean. We are part of the ocean of Existence. We just have to trust that everything is going perfectly because Existence is in charge, and we are one with Existence. In this way we stay above the line of negativity and passivity. We stay compassionate, in love and compassion. We don't cross the border into sympathy, which causes us to feel bad or worry about others. With compassion, anytime we are in contact with others, they will feel our love, and they will become calm and feel free.

The most important qualities of a person on the path of mysticism are flexibility and trust. When a mystic hears the truth, the ego drops, and without the ego we become one with Existence. Anytime we surrender the ego, we become one with Existence. With oneness, we become joyful and loving. This joyful and loving feeling gives us freedom. A mystic is flexible. Because they feel so free, they don't get stuck in their ideas or thoughts. They flow with whatever is happening. They trust whatever is.

PAINTINGS
by Sharam

VIEW AND PURCHASE GICLÉE PRINTS

VISIT:
Sharam.org

www.ingramcontent.com/pod-product-compliance
Lightning Source LLC
Chambersburg PA
CBHW041551220426
43666CB00002B/30